Anxiety in Relationships

How to Stop Anxiety, Negative Thinking And Control your Thoughts

Emily White

Introduction

Relationships. They have their ups and downs, happy moments and sad moments, obstacles and challenges. No relationship is perfect and nearly every type of relationship out there takes work to maintain. But what if those relationships had an extra element to deal with? An element that causes distress, panic attacks, worries, frustrations, feelings of isolation, and loneliness? What if the relationships that you form had to deal with an element that put an extra strain on those relationships?

That element is none other than anxiety. It is a prevalent disorder that affects millions of people around the world. If you thought you were the only one having to struggle through this, think again. Struggling with relationship anxiety is more common than you realize

With the right coping strategies, your relationships no longer have to struggle through the consequences of this condition. Your relationships can experience the happiness that you long for. Working together with the people you love, you can achieve positive changes in your relationship. Anxiety may be a difficult condition to deal with, but it is a condition that can be overcome through persistence and perseverance.

What Is Anxiety?

Anxiety is a reaction of agitation, such as discomfort or fright, that can be slight or grave. Each person has moods of anxiety at around instant in their life. Falling and being in love challenges us in various and numerous ways. A number of these challenges are unexpected, and when we face them the first time, our human nature makes us defensive. For example, if you love somebody without question, and he/she makes you extremely upset, odds are, you will try not to be defenseless. On an individual point, we as a whole dread being hurt, deliberately, or unknowingly. Unexpectedly, this dread develops to raise when we are making sure about what we plan. On the off chance that a relationship is acceptable, one begins to fear the 'effect of a separation.' Consequently, he/she begins to take the protection, make a separation, and cut off the association in the long run. If we are encountering love and being treated in an uncommonly decent manner, we become tense.

That defensive tension becomes a barrier. It is important to note that anxiety in a relationship does not only arise because of the things going between the two parties involved. This feeling may also arise because of our perception. The things you tell yourself about a relationship, love, attraction, desire, et cetera will affect our lives. This means that you might have the best partner in the world, but your thoughts still hinder you from realizing it and enjoying the moment. The proverbial 'Inner voice' is very dangerous if it is negative.

This mental couch can tell us things that fuel our fear of intimacy. The critical inner voice can feed us lousy advice such as "You are too ugly for him/her," "Even the other people have left you before," "You cannot trust such a man/woman."

What do such thoughts do? They make us turn against the people we love and, most importantly, ourselves. The critical inner voice can make us hostile, paranoid, and unnecessarily suspicious. It can also drive our feelings of defensiveness, distrust, anxiety, and jealousy to unhealthy levels. This tiny negative voice feeds us an endless stream of unhealthy thoughts that make us worried about relationships and undermine our happiness. It prevents us from enjoying life wholesomely.

The main challenge comes in once we focus on these thoughts. We get into our heads and focus on whatever that minute thought is saying. Then we process it and ponder it and roast and re-roast it until it appears like an unmovable mountain. At that moment, one is distracted from his/her partner, thus no real relation and interaction. After brewing over the thoughts, one might start to act out, either immaturely or in destructive ways. For instance, one might start to boss the partner around, monitoring all his/her moves, making unnecessary nasty comments, ignoring, or mistreating the other.

Supposing your partner stays late at work or passes by the local bar for a drink before coming home. The critical inner thought will trigger thoughts such as "where is he/she? What is he doing?" with who and why? Does she/he [prefer to be away from home? Maybe he/she doesn't love me anymore." These opinions can run through your mind so much that by the time your partner gets home, you are feeling completely insecure, paranoid, furious, and defensive. In this state, it becomes hard to have a constructive conversation about his/her whereabouts.

Consequently, this partner will feel misunderstood and frustrated. Furthermore, he/she will also take a defensive stance. Soon, the dynamic of the relationship shifts from pleasure and comfort to irrational and unfair treatments; instead of enjoying the rest of the evening, it becomes wasted as everyone feels withdrawn and upset.

Do you realize that in such a case, you have effectively created the distance you initially feared? O you also realize that your partner might have had no harmful intentions. The fact is, the distance you have created was not caused by the situation itself or circumstances. No. It was triggered by that critical inner voice, which might have been wrong. That voice colored your thinking with negativity, distorted your perception, and in the end, led you to self- destruction.

The biggest challenge that leads us to self-destruction in relationships is self- doubt. If we assess most of the things we worry about in a relationship, we realize that we can handle the consequences. The majority of us are resilient enough to experience heartbreaks and heal. It probably has happened before, and you did not die from it. However, our inner voice tends to blow things out of proportion, especially the negative ones. That voice terrorizes and catastrophizes everything making it hard to stay rational. It can trigger severe anxiety spells over some non-existent relationship dynamics that do not exist and strange, intangible threats. Probably, breakups would not be so painful if we did not have that critical voice. It is the thing that analyses things and tears us apart by pointing out all our flaws and things we failed to do. The distorted reality makes us think that we are not healthy and resilient enough to survive. That critical voice is the cynical friend who is always giving bad advice "You cannot survive a heartbreak, just stay guarded and do not become vulnerable."

We form our defenses depending on unique life experiences and adaptations. The inner voice also borrows from those unique experiences. If a former partner said that he/she would leave you because you are overweight or underweight, the inner voice would use that line to distort reality. It will make you think that another partner is noticing the same flaws and that he/she will leave because of them. When feeling insecure or anxious, some of us tend to become desperate or clingy in our actions. Others become control freaks, wanting to possess the partner. Many people start to feel crowded, like there is no breathing space in the relationship, thus choosing to distance themselves from their loved ones.

In extreme cases, we detach from the feelings of desire in their relationship. We can start to be aloof, guarded, or wholly withdrawn. Such patterns of attachment and relating can come from our early life experiences. In childhood years, we develop attachment patterns unconsciously, depending on our environment. The patterns become the model for our adult life. They influence how we assess our needs and how we get them fulfilled. These attachment patterns and styles are the main determinants of anxiety one feels in a relationship.

Understanding the difference between normal sensations of anxiety and an anxiety disorder calling for clinical attention can help individuals identify and treat the problem. Everybody feels distressed now and then. It's a normal emotion. For example, you may contact worried when faced with trouble at the office before taking a test or making a vital choice.

Stress and anxiety conditions are different, though. They are a group of mental diseases, and the distress they trigger can maintain you from carrying on with your life regularly. For individuals who have one, worry and anxiety are constant and frustrating and can be disabling. However, with therapy, many individuals can take care of those sensations and get back to a satisfying life. When an individual encounters possibly harmful or distressing triggers, feelings of stress and anxiety are not just typical but necessary for survival.

Since the earliest days of humankind, the predators' method and incoming threat trigger alarms in the body and permits incredibly elusive activity.

These alarm systems become noticeable in the form of an elevated heartbeat, sweating, and boosted level of sensitivity to environments. The risk causes a rush of adrenalin, a hormone, and chemical messenger in mind, which triggers these anxious responses in a procedure called the "fight-or-flight' reaction. This prepares people to physically confront or leave any type of potential hazards to safety and security.

For many individuals, ranging from bigger pets and an impending threat is a much less important issue than it would have been for very early human beings. Stress and anxieties currently revolve around the job, cash, domesticity, wellness, and other important issues that demand a person's focus without always calling for the 'fight-or-flight' response.

Before a vital life occasion or throughout a difficult situation, the anxious sensation is an all-natural echo of the initial 'fight-or-flight' reaction. It can still be essential to survival-- anxiety about being struck by a car when crossing the street, as an example, means that an individual will naturally look at both methods to avoid the threat.

Stress and anxiety are your body's all-natural actions to stress and anxiety. It's a sensation of concern or worry concerning what's ahead. Going to a job interview or providing a speech might trigger many people to feel scared and worried about the institution's first day. Yet if your feelings of stress and anxiety are severe, last for longer than six months, and are hindering your life, you might have an anxiety condition.

The period or extent of a distressed feeling can, in some cases, be out of proportion to the original trigger or stress factor. Physical signs and symptoms, such as raised blood pressure as well as nausea, may also develop. These responses move beyond stress and anxiety into a stress and anxiety condition. The APA defines a person with an anxiety disorder as "having persisting invasive thoughts or problems." As soon as stress and anxiety get to the disease stage, it can hinder daily function.

It's typical to feel distressed about transferring to a brand-new area, beginning a brand-new job, or taking a test. This sort of tension is undesirable. However, it might rouse you to work more troublesomely and to improve work. Normal nervousness is an impression that reoccurs; nonetheless, it doesn't meddle with your regular day to day existence. When it comes to an anxiousness condition, the feeling of fear may be with you at all times. It is intense and also often crippling.

This kind of anxiety may trigger you to stop doing things you appreciate. It might prevent you from going into an elevator, going across the street, or even leaving your home in extreme cases. If left neglected, the anxiety will undoubtedly keep getting worse. Anxiousness problems are one of the most usual types of mental illness and can influence any person at any type of age. Concurring to the American Psychiatric Organization, ladies are extra likely than men to be identified with an anxiousness problem.

Understanding Anxiety in Relationship

Worry. Uncertainty. Distress. It feels like the weight of the world is resting on your shoulders. Happiness seems like an eternal struggle, and even when you do experience a little bit of happiness, the moment seems fleeting. You long to form connections and bonds with others, and yet you're worried about all the ways the relationship could go wrong. You worry about whether the relationships you form are real. You worry about whether they are going to last. You worry about whether the other person cares for you as much as you care for them. To other people, your fears seem irrational, and they cannot understand why your fears over what they perceive to be trivial seem to plague you consistently.

But your fears are not irrational. Not even a little bit. Your fears stem from a genuine problem, and that problem is anxiety. Oh yes, relationship anxiety is something a lot of people struggle with. Even if everything is going wonderful and great in the relationship, these persistent fears refuse to leave your troubled mind. It continues to plague you, eat away at you, and you keep finding faults in your relationship and reasons to worry, even when there is nothing to worry about. Every single day, you're worried that the relationship is not going to last, and this fear could potentially lead to you self-sabotaging your relationships in the end. You're so worried that it's not going to last that your actions begin to manifest these troubled thoughts and before you know it, your relationship has come to a halt.

Do I Have Relationship Anxiety?

Do all the symptoms above sound all too familiar to you? You could be dealing with relationship anxiety, and if you weren't sure before, these are the telltale signs that will indicate if this is indeed the case:

• Your Constant Insecurity About Your Relationship Is Destructive - Insecurity is one of the most common ways relationship anxiety manifests itself. Sometimes, it feels like you're driving yourself crazy believing that you have no real place in their lives. You're always stressed that the people in your life are going to leave you as soon as they have a reason to, and this can be for any relationship you have in your life, not specifically romantic relationships alone. You're always wondering exactly how much you matter to them, and how important you are. You know you would do anything for them, but you're not convinced they would do the same for you no matter how many times they try to reassure you. Your thoughts can be so destructive that you question whether the connection you have with them is real.

• You're Constantly Doubting Their Feelings for You - This one is applicable to romantic relationships in particular. You find yourself routinely doubting if your partner's feelings are real. They could reassure you that they love you 100 times a day and you would still doubt and question if they mean what they said. They could make the biggest, grandest romantic gestures in the world, like proclaiming their love for you with a blimp shouting the words across the sky and you would *still* find yourself doubting. You don't want to feel this way, but it is almost as though your anxiety has a mind of its own. Once it takes over, it's hard to ignore. No matter how much they reassure you that they love you, it is never going to be enough for your anxious mind. You always need proof that you are the only one for them. Anxiety has given you a deep-seated fear of abandonment. You want an absolute guarantee that they will never leave you.

• You Depend On Them Too Much - Are you attached to your phone because you're waiting for a text back from your partner? Do you start feeling those anxious nerves bubbling up inside you when they take too long to text you back? If you go too long without seeing them, you start to worry that they're going to forget about you or find someone else (even though they won't). They've told you that they're busy and they might not be able to reply that often, but you still worry and fret anyway. When they spend time with anyone else other than you, you feel upset. Although it is natural to feel a strong attachment to your partner and an equally strong desire to spend as much time as possible as you can with them, your relationship anxiety is making you needy and paranoid. You find yourself becoming overly dependent on your significant other.

● Your Strong Desire to Please Them Is Unhealthy - You find yourself keeping quiet and not wanting to speak up about the things that bother you, even when you know you should. You keep quiet because you want to avoid any disagreements or conflicts that you believe might jeopardize your relationship. You choose to keep quiet, even when it is eating away at you. You've convinced yourself that the best thing to do is to go along with whatever your partner wants, even though it is eating away at you. Not speaking your mind is making you feel distressed, but you don't want to do anything about it. Does this sound familiar?

That's because you have relationship anxiety. This deep-seated fear of losing your partner has led you to believe that if you don't do everything you can to please your partner, they are going to leave you. You keep going above and beyond for them, even if it makes you unhappy to do it.

• You Find Yourself Overanalyzing Everything About Your Relationship - How often do you replay in your mind the things that go on in your relationship? How many times do you replay past conversations in your head and then beat yourself up over the things you wish you had said. Every little disagreement haunts you, and it continues to eat away at you long after the conversation is over. It bothers you so much, in fact, that it becomes a full-blown worry that your partner is going to leave you because of the disagreement.

• Everything Feels Like a Reason to Beat Yourself Up - Maybe you forgot to greet your partner this morning. Perhaps you overlooked something they asked you to help them out with. Maybe you couldn't make it out on a date this weekend, or you missed their call because you didn't hear your phone ring while you were out buying lunch. No matter what the reason, big or small, it seems like a valid reason to beat yourself up over. You keep replaying in your mind all the ways you've convinced yourself that you failed as a partner. Every little mistake that you make seems like a valid reason to be angry with yourself. Every little mistake seems like a good reason to worry that it is going to be the end of your relationship. No matter how much your partner tells you it's okay and that it is no big deal, their words hold no meaning. You still beat yourself up anyway and do it repeatedly in your mind, feeling worse about yourself each time that you do. Guilt, remorse, regret, and worry are the emotions that plague you daily and it seems impossible to shake them.

• You're Afraid of Getting Too Serious - You long for a serious, committed relationship. At the same time, you're terrified by the idea of getting too serious with your partner. Why? You're worried that they're going to leave you and break your heart. You love them yet find it hard to commit to them because you're so scared of having your heartbroken that you have built a wall around yourself. That wall has become so thick it's impossible for anyone to get close to you. You long for a committed relationship, but you're afraid of it at the same time. This internal war going on inside you is emotionally distressing, and you feel all alone because you believe no one understands what you are going through. You might be right too since not everyone is going to understand why you worry this way. Relationship anxiety is going to make it difficult for you to get close to anyone, not just your partner either. Friendships and getting close to people is always going to feel like a tremendous challenge. Being alone and heartbroken is a thought that terrifies you so much you keep people at an emotional distance, including the person that you love. To you, it is only a matter of time before your relationship falls apart and all your worst fears come true.

● You're Always Waiting for The Other Shoe to Drop - It feels like you are always on the edge of your seat, wondering when the relationship is going to come to an end. You're waiting for a disaster to strike or waiting for the other shoe to drop. Thanks to your relationship anxiety, you have become convinced that you are going to be hurt and disappointed. It's just a matter of time and anxiously anticipating that moment is stopping you from enjoying the happiness that you should have in your relationship. When your partner makes a mistake, you immediately latch onto that as a possible reason that the relationship is doomed to fail. You find it hard to let go of their mistakes and overthink every little thing that they say. You know it is not healthy to do this, but you can't help yourself. The smallest of issues turn into full- blown arguments. You think you're protecting yourself by being on your guard, waiting for something to go wrong, but what you're really doing is self-sabotaging your relationship.

Relationship anxiety is going to hold you back from happiness, from being present and enjoying the special moments' other people enjoy with their significant others. If nothing is done about this, your relationship is not going to have the fighting chance that it needs to survive. Being in a relationship is no doubt a wonderful feeling, knowing that you have someone to love and that someone feels the same way about you. But at the same time, a relationship is not without its challenges, and for someone with anxiety, those challenges are magnified tenfold.

The Common Causes Behind Your Anxious Feelings

Your childhood could have something to do with why you experience anxiety in relationships. It ties back to the attachment that we form with our caregivers. These could be our parents, guardians, other family members, or anyone who had a major influence on you while you were growing up. The relationships we form from childhood have a major impact on us, more so than we realize. Since these early relationships had a big influence on our upbringing and these are the relationships we have been exposed to for years, it will have an influence on the relationships we go on to form outside the family. It will influence the adult relationships you form, from friendships to romantic relationships. In fact, our subconscious mind uses these romantic relationships we form to replace those attachments we formed in our early years.

This explains why we have a deep longing to be connected with someone. Even if we don't want to admit it, no one wants to be alone. Loneliness is one of the most depressing feelings a person could suffer. Once we grow up and forge our own path in life, the subconscious part of our brain still seeks attachment to others, and thus, we try to form relationships outside our familial comfort. This then leads to a strong desire of people-pleasing, and that explains why relationship anxiety can be the cause of trying to bend over backward too much to please your partner until your own happiness is jeopardized. People-pleasers usually do what they do because they have unresolved abandonment issues or an unsatisfied need for love. This explains why you frequently put the needs of others before your own, because you're so terrified of losing those relationships that you would do anything to keep them, even at the cost of your own happiness.

Here are some of the common reasons why we experience anxiety:

• We Overthink - Sometimes referred to as rumination, overthinking is when you get so caught up in your own thoughts you can't focus on anything else. Everything feels like a big deal, and every experience and interaction becomes negative because your anxious thoughts are clouding your judgment. The inability to let things go and sweating the small stuff is a clear sign of overthinking. If your obsessive thoughts are keeping you up at night, then you're dealing with anxiety.

• We Try to Overachieve - The thrill of achieving something can be addictive, and no doubt accomplishments are a good thing. But if trying to reach these accomplishments gives you anxiety throughout the entire process, is it worth the distress? In the long-run, the answer is no. That is because anxiety is a stressful emotion, and anytime you put your body through unnecessary stress, you're hurting it. When you're overworked and stressed out all the time, that only makes you more susceptible to anxiety and depression. Striving for unrealistically high goals is only setting yourself up for failure and disappointment, which is not helpful for your anxiety.

• We Struggle With Low Self-Esteem - In today's world, popularity comes with a cost. That cost is your privacy. Social media has piled on the pressure of feeling like we constantly need to go above and beyond to impress people we barely know, let alone speak to in real life. Some people make it a point to keep up with appearances on social media, believing that this platform defines who they are. If you're someone who struggles with anxiety, the desire to be liked and accepted on these social platforms is magnified. The pressure to be liked by others can mess with your mind. When you post a picture or an update but don't get the likes and responses you hoped that you would, your emotions take a nosedive. This explains why one of the most common causes of negative self-image is linked to social media.

• We're Prone to Pessimistic Thinking - Pessimistic and negative thinking is like a mental prison for those who struggle with anxiety. They don't want to be in this prison, yet at the same time find it difficult to break free. They're trapped in their own negative thoughts and this makes it extremely difficult to develop that optimistic outlook needed to feel happy with their lives. You're always worried about the worst-case scenario. It feels like nothing can ever go right. There always seems to be something new to worry about, and the smallest inconveniences become a reason to spiral downwards into depression and misery. It is a mental prison that is difficult to escape.

• We Experience Some Kind of Traumatic Event - Any kind of traumatic experience you might have gone through in the past has a big role to play in shaping your fears and anxieties. Traumatic moments leave a lasting impact, and at times, they could become the reason why you developed anxiety, to begin with. Our minds are built for self-preservation, and traumatic moments make us want to avoid any kind of situation that could potentially traumatize us all over again. This sense of self-preservation is so strong it is the reason why we develop phobias. If you find yourself feeling anxious for no apparent reason, it could be because you've experienced some deep-seated trauma in the past that has left a bigger scar on you than you realized. There could be lingering issues from past experiences that you still need to resolve.

• New Experiences Frighten Us - Stepping out of your comfort zone is never an easy thing to deal with. For some people, the very idea of undergoing new experiences is enough to act as an anxiety-trigger. Stepping out of your comfort zone requires a great deal of courage, but change that is sudden and stressful can be scary. The problem is that change is one of the many constants in life, and if you don't learn to embrace it, it is always going to act as a trigger for your anxiety to spiral out of control.

The Fear of Falling in Love

Love is a wonderful thing, yet at the same time, it can be a terrifying thing because there is always a risk of having your heart broken into a million pieces. Falling in love and investing all your emotions in another person can be a scary prospect for anyone, but for those dealing with relationship anxiety, that fear is a hundred times worse in their mind. We all experience worry at some point in our lives because those types of emotions are both natural and unavoidable. Even the happiest people in the world worry from time to time. There is always something to worry about. You worry about paying your bills, you worry about your family, you worry about your job, your health, and the list could go on. You worry, your partner worries, your friends worry, your colleagues at work worry, your family worries, everybody worries from time to time. But relationship anxiety is a whole different kind of worry.

Relationship anxiety can lead to a genuine fear of falling in love called *philophobia.* This is a very real problem, and people struggling with *philophobia* often experience overwhelming emotions when they are on the brink of falling in love. Feelings of uneasiness, apprehension, fear, and worry that is triggered when a person is faced with falling in love with someone and dealing with anxiety only makes the situation feel a lot worse. Combined with *philophobia,* they could become abnormally anxious or nervous, and the mere thought of falling in love with their partner could cause them to either self-sabotage the relationship or run away altogether. This problem goes beyond commitment or trust issues.

Here is an example of what anxiety and *philophobia* might look like. When you first start dating, everything is going well. But then, your partner confronts you about pulling away and becoming distant in the relationship. Without realizing it, your fight or flight response has kicked in, and you find it difficult to explain why you're pulling away despite the obvious interest and feelings you have for your partner. Relationship anxiety is a very real problem that many couples are struggling with and it can do real harm to a relationship if not properly dealt with. It is not just about the fear of commitment and getting into a relationship in the beginning, but it can also continue throughout the relationship at various stages and has been known to sometimes get worse the more serious a relationship gets. When confronted about your commitment issues, you could resort to becoming defensive, lying about your commitment issues when you're convinced they are not going to understand, and pulling away from your partner even before when your anxieties and fears have taken control. Without meaning to, you're going to subconsciously do everything you can to avoid getting too intimate.

Philophobia sounds a lot like social anxiety disorder, but there is a difference. Those dealing with social anxiety disorder tend to feel nervous and avoid social situations. People with *philophobia*, on the other hand, only display signs of anxiousness in certain circumstances. For example, when trying to form a lasting romantic relationship. As irrational as your fears may seem to others, the truth is, you're simply trying to avoid inflicting more pain on yourself. You want to love and be loved in return, but you're so afraid of having your heartbroken that you can't bring yourself to be open to love anymore. It isn't easy living a life in which you are constantly worried and afraid that something bad is going to happen. When it involves someone that you care about, it can be almost unbearable because of the very thought and idea of losing the one that you love is too painful to bear. Taking a leap of faith to find the love you so desperately seek in your life feels like a leap that is too big to make. After the breakdown of a relationship, anxiety can make it difficult for you to move on and deal with it.

Living with Relationship Anxiety Can Be Immensely Stressful Imagine having a fear that is so great it stops you from forming relationships. The love and companionship that every single person in this world craves is something you want more than anything, but at the same time, feels impossible to get because of the condition you're dealing with. You feel completely alone, and you feel like no one understands what you are going through. When you're dealing with anxiety, it's hard to explain your fears. Others might say you're overreacting or that your fears are irrational, but to you, these fears are very real. Anxiety is as real as all your other human emotions, and this means that it is going to vary in intensity depending on the individual. Just like how the other emotions you experience would vary in intensity. People who are dealing with relationship anxiety are susceptible to experiencing a wide range of symptoms over the course of their relationship. Sometimes, the symptoms could manifest physically, for example:

An increase in your heart rate. Sweating profusely all of a sudden. Feeling nauseous or anxious.

Difficulty breathing and moments that can be associated with a panic attack.

You feel like you are drowning or suffocating, unable to cope because you feel so overwhelmed.

Trouble sleeping at night.

Your mind is constantly worrying and stressing out about something even though nothing may actually be happening.

Sweaty palms and butterflies in your stomach.

Anxiety can have such a negative impact on a relationship. In some extreme cases, your fear can become so great that you become a recluse, preferring not to have any bond with the outside world because you can't bear to take that risk. Relationship anxiety is incredibly complicated to deal with because you are handling not just one or two, but several emotional ranges. Loneliness can be a very dangerous emotion for someone who is already dealing with relationship anxiety, leading to possible depression or substance abuse in some extreme cases.

Is there a way out for someone dealing with relationship anxiety? There is, with a lot of hard work. If you are dealing with relationship anxiety, all hope is not lost. Not yet, at least. There is a way to overcome your struggles, and that is why you're reading this book right now. You *want* to seek a solution to your problem, and you have already made a remarkable step in the right direction. You have acknowledged that there is a problem and you are ready to fix it. It is possible to rid your life of the anxiety that is weighing down your relationship before it is too late as long as you are willing to work on it, but you are going to need the help of your partner too. You cannot do this alone because a relationship involves two people, and two lives that are being affected by anxiety, even though you may be the one who is going through it. You need to be prepared to be open and honest with your partner if the two of you are going to work together to rebuild your relationship, and it is important that both you and your partner remain patient throughout this process. It is going to take time and miracles are not going to happen overnight.

Why and How Anxiety Can Take Over Relationship

Before anxiety affects your relationship, it affects something else first. *Your brain.* Anxiety is the brain's way of telling us that we need to watch out for danger. From an evolutionary standpoint, this certainly came in handy when our ancestors were living in the wild, fighting for survival against nature's predators. However, the brain has not evolved from this self-defense mechanism, even though the lives that we lead today are completely different.

<u>A Look at The Anxious Brain</u>

You're all too familiar with how anxiety feels like. Everyone has had experience in this aspect because we have all experienced anxiety at some point in our lives. The only difference is that for some people, the anxiety never diminishes or goes away, even when the perceived danger has passed. We do need a little bit of anxiety in our lives from time to time because anxiety keeps us alive. Without it, we would all be in serious trouble. Anxious thoughts stem from the mind's tendency to obsess and pinpoint all the things that can, might, and could possibly go wrong. When the brain interprets something as dangerous and then tells us to avoid this danger at all costs, there's a rush of relief the brain gets when it believes it has avoided a potentially dangerous situation. For example, when the brain perceives this new person you are about to start dating as "dangerous" because they could break your heart, it convinces you to build a wall to protect yourself from getting hurt. But the brain doesn't stop there. It keeps reminding you of the danger of having your heart broken until eventually, your anxiety and worries get the best of you. The result? You subconsciously self-sabotage what might have been a wonderful relationship.

Anxiety started off as a natural and helpful emotion that kept us alive as a species for as long as we have. But in today's context, anxiety prevents us from living our lives to the fullest. We're surrounded by more stressful stimuli today than we have ever been, and this has only made the situation worse. The human brain hates uncertainty. It doesn't take kindly to unknown variables and any element that is out of its control. That's why worrying about life, in general, is a major cause of anxiety. This is why anxiety sufferers and over-thinkers find the prospect of the future so alarming. The fear of the unknown happens to be all the fuel their brain needs to start working overtime churning out one negative thought after another.

When your brain senses what it believes to be a danger to you, your amygdala is triggered. It kicks in and gets your body ready to react, putting it in a state known as the *fight or flight* response. This reaction goes back millions of years to our very first human ancestors. They had to keep their amygdala sensitive to danger to give themselves the best chance of staying alive.

Over the next few generations, the anxious part of our brain would continue to play its role until eventually it was given the name *anxiety*. Anxiety on its own is not all bad. It only becomes a problem when there is no immediate threat but your amygdala continues telling your body and your brain that you are in danger. This is when anxiety becomes a problem when your brain is unable to distinguish between what is genuinely dangerous and what isn't. Our instinct is to survive when we're faced with any kind of physical danger. The fight or flight response kicks in when triggered by what the brain perceives as any kind of danger, and the body begins churning out the adrenalin you need to give you the required energy and strength to get yourself out of that dangerous situation. When we are confronted, there are only two ways we will choose to respond. We will either stand our ground and confront the danger or we will flee.

Today, the brain has a hard time distinguishing what is really dangerous, but that is not entirely its fault. With the hectic lifestyles, we lead today, almost everything could be perceived as "danger" when those factors happen to trigger our anxiety. If your job makes you anxious, your fight or flight response is unknowingly triggered and you could spend almost an entire day with high levels of adrenaline and cortisol in your body.

Why Anxiety Is No Good for Your Love Life

Besides the fact that it is going to disrupt your ability to form strong relationships when all you think about is the many ways it could go wrong, anxiety is not good for us because the human body was not meant to store these hormones for prolonged periods, and doing so could have long-term damaging effects physically. When the stress response is chronically present and remains active because of the prolonged stressful periods we endure, it can cause significant wear and tear on our bodies, physically and emotionally. When our anxiety is triggered, we feel stuck and hopeless. We try to avoid these situations that make us uncomfortable, the same way our ancestors avoided the predators in the wild. But this reaction can cause problems when those triggers are an important part of life, like going to school or work, meeting new people, and forming new relationships.

There is nothing wrong with you. Your brain is only trying to help in the best way it knows how by triggering your amygdala. It is trying to help when it believes you're in danger. There are several reasons why our bodies are not meant to be in this prolonged state of anxiety, among which include leading to sleep difficulties, where you have trouble falling asleep, and wake up frequently in between. Profuse sweating or cold sweats, feeling like you've got "pins and needles" in your joints, upset stomach and digestive problems, frequent headaches, and migraines, dizziness and nausea, difficulty concentrating, feeling dehydrated and extremely thirsty all the time, and feeling overwhelmed and exhausted are just some of the many symptoms associated with prolonged anxiety. None of which are good for the body.

Despite what people may try to tell you about anxiety being "no big deal" or that you will "get over it" with time, anxiety is a very serious condition that is not to be taken lightly. If left untreated, there's a real risk of anxiety developing into severe depression and eventually suicide when it feels like you can no longer take it anymore. If you're really struggling to cope, never be dismissive of your problems or view it lightly. Anxiety can be treated with the right techniques, support, but of course, you can only seek the help that you need if you are willing to admit anxiety is becoming a very real problem in your life. Struggling with a mental disorder is nothing to be ashamed of.

<u>What It's Like to Date When You Have Anxiety</u>

When you have anxiety, dating is not going to be a walk in the park. When anxiety is your reality, it can feel like you are all alone in this world. There have probably been many times in your relationship where you wondered why your partner is with you when they could be with someone better. There will be a lot of negative thoughts swimming around your head about your relationship, and typically, the thought patterns always hover on the negative side and reflect their feelings of fear and worry.

Anxiety is not fun. It has ruined social experiences, relationships, even the ability to function in an ordinary routine for those who have a more severe type of anxiety disorder. Anxiety is different for everyone, and not all of the points below might be something you can relate to. However, this does not mean that your experience with anxiety is any less valid. Your experience with anxiety is as valid as anyone else's, and for those who are reading this because they are trying to understand their anxious partner better, this is what it's like to date when you struggle with anxiety:

• Saying "Don't Worry About It" Does Not Help - Anxiety is not a switch you can turn on and off. Just because someone tells you "not to worry about it," it doesn't mean you can. You are already trying your best to cope in the best way your know-how. Don't blame yourself or feel bad that you can't "stop worrying" just because someone told you to do it.
They don't understand what you are going through.

• You're Always Feeling Self-Conscious - You feel this way even around your partner. You feel like they might be watching your every move, waiting for you to slip up and make a mistake. One aspect that comes with anxiety is the fear of being judged. When you're in a relationship and you're dealing with anxiety, there is a constant and persistent worry that your partner is going to eventually leave you one day when they realize how "flawed" you are. You worry about the way you look and act, and you worry about what your partner is thinking of you.

• It Affects Your Ability to Be Calm Around Your Partner - You don't want to be in a constant state of panic and freak out over every little thing, yet it almost feels as if you can't help yourself. Try as you might, you find yourself getting worked up, worried, distressed, and emotional around your partner. They try their best to get you to stay calm, but you still find yourself prone to hysterical outbursts. The smallest of issues can seem like massive triggers and a cause for alarm.

• It Feels Almost Impossible to Open Up to Your Partner – You want to become closer to your partner, yet you can't seem to bring your guard down. Each time you try and make an effort to get close to them or let them in a little bit more, your anxiety immediately causes you to close up again. Anxiety complicates your relationship, making you feel tense and uneasy at the very thought of allowing yourself to be vulnerable in front of your partner. You come off as aloof or distant, even though that is not what you want to be at all. Familiarity doesn't make these worries and fears go away either. No matter how much you love your partner, the fear and distress are always lingering at the back of your mind.

● You Sometimes Make Excuses to Avoid Your Partner - When your anxiety feels like it is too much to be around other people, including your partner, you start making excuses to avoid them. You would rather hide in your room than go out with them. This is how serious anxiety can become. It doesn't matter how much you love them, how much you want to be around them, or whether you're supposed to be celebrating a special occasion. When your anxiety feels like it is too much to bear, the only escape seems to be complete and utter avoidance

How to Date Despite the Anxiety

When you have anxiety, it's easy to feel overwhelmed all the time. When you're obsessed about the smallest, possible detail that may seem insignificant to your partner, you're bound to feel tired by all those emotions. As a result of all that overthinking, you get worked up and feel that you are unable to cope because you can't think straight and think rationally in the situation. When your emotions are all over the place, you'll feel tired easily and crash and burn often. You're probably feeling tired all the time too. Anxiety is a very draining emotion, and no one can truly understand how much it can impact a person unless they themselves are dealing with anxiety. This is why those who are dealing with anxiety feel tired so easily because their mind is overworked, constantly worrying every waking minute, stressing, and obsessing about their fears and worries.

Does that mean dating is impossible? Not at all. Dating while you have anxiety is still possible, as long as you have the right coping techniques to help you stay strong when you need it most:

• Stay Present - When you tend to overthink and blow things out of proportion, your mind can make a mountain out of a molehill. You start getting ahead of yourself, worrying about the future, trying to produce solutions that no one has the answers to. Why? Because we cannot predict the future. Worrying about what might happen in the future is only going to make you feel worse. As difficult as it may be, try your best to take deep, measured breaths whenever you feel your anxiety rising. Remind yourself as you breathe deeply to focus on the present. Focus on what is happening *here* and what is happening *right now,* because the present moment is the only thing that matters. Hold on to the present reality. If it is not happening in the present, then remind yourself there is no need to jump several steps ahead and worry about nothing. Don't try to predict the future, because that is something no one can do.

• Look For What You Can Touch and Smell - A good tip to help you stay focused on the present is to look for things that you can touch. Your mind needs something specific to focus on that serves as a distraction from your anxious thoughts. Look around and pick five items that you can physically touch. A book, a pen, a piece of paper, your phone, your coffee mug. It could be anything as long as you can touch it, it's real. Once you have focused on what you can touch, try to look for five things that you can smell. Doing this forces your brain to interrupt its own hectic train of thought by focusing on something else.

• Recall the Positive Things You Feel In Your Relationship - When you're struggling to find something else to focus on besides your anxiety, think about all the things that you love about your partner and how they make you feel. What positive emotions do you feel when you see them smile? When they make you breakfast? How do you feel when they give you a big hug and remind you that they love you?

• Have Direction and Intention - One of the reasons why you have anxiety is because you want to have a sense of control. When you lack that sense of control, that is when your thoughts start going off in all different directions. Having a direction and intention gives you that sense of control your anxious brain is craving. For example, be intentional about what you plan to do with your partner if you know you're meeting them tomorrow. Think about the direction you want that day to go, what you would like to do, what you want to talk about, anything that is within your control, you can focus on that. It gives you a sense of control because you know what you want to do and how you want the day to play out. You're making plans and not leaving up to chance. These guidelines help you feel like you're in control, minimizing the uncertainty that triggers your anxiety.

● Talk to People You Can Trust - When you get too caught up in your own thoughts, it can be easy to lose perspective. If you feel like you need to talk to someone other than your partner, don't be afraid to reach out to people you can trust. Limit the people you approach just one or two because reaching out to too many can cause even more overthinking at times. Everyone is going to have a different opinion and having too many opinions could create even more confusion for your already anxious mind. Talk to people who have your best interest and heart, people who know you're struggling with anxiety. Avoid being alone with your own thoughts because you could become so worked up you end up lashing out at your partner when it could easily be avoided. The last thing you want is to trigger an argument.

● You Are Deserving and You Are Enough - Anxiety can instill a lot of fear in you. One of the biggest challenges you face when you're trying to date while you manage your anxiety is the challenge of believing you are worthy. Anxiety can make you feel like less of a person, that you somehow don't deserve love because there is "something wrong" with you. That is not true at all, not even a little bit. *You are enough, you are worthy, and you deserve all the love in the world.* No one in this world is perfect. If they're not struggling with anxiety, they have their own demons to battle. But does this make them any less worthy of love? Not at all. In fact, you should be given even *more* love from those who have a lot of love to give. You are brave for trying to open your heart to another even with the struggles you're going through, and you should feel proud.

Possible Causes of a Relationship Anxiety

Most times, relationship anxiety could be a manifestation of a deep-rooted problem. Here are the common causes of relationship anxiety:

Complicated Relationship

When you are uncertain about your relationship, or it is not clearly defined, it can be classified as complicated. This applies to those that are dating. For instance, a woman may not know the man's intentions - whether he wants to marry her or is just in it for fun. Also, a long-distance relationship could result in anxiety. In such cases, partners must learn to trust each other.

Comparison

Comparing your current relationship with past ones should be avoided as much as possible. You might begin to entertain feelings of regret if you discover that your past relationship was better in the areas of finance, communication, sex, and other aspects. To avoid this feeling, you should never compare your marriage or relationship with others or those you have had in the past.

Constant Fighting

When you are always quarreling with your partner, you might never stop worrying because you don't know when the ensuing altercation will crop up. This is one of the causes of severe anxiety in a relationship because your bid to avoid quarreling will not allow you to have a pleasant time with your partner.

Lack Of Understanding

Partners that do not take the time to understand each other will always face difficulties. As mentioned earlier, the constant quarreling will result in an uneasy relationship. Are you noticing the symptoms of anxiety coupled with miscommunications? The absence of understanding might be the reason for your relationship anxiety. Get to know your partner better and encourage them to know you.

Other Issues

Difficult experiences in past unhealthy relationships might result in many other issues. Not only that, neglect during childhood, abuse in the past, and lack of affection are reasons why someone can feel anxious in a relationship.

Once you have identified your relationship issue's root cause, getting rid of it will be the following step. Do not forget that the primary reason for the self- evaluation of any problem is getting rid of it.

Getting Over Relationship Insecurity

Everyone feels nervous when they are about to start a new relationship. You hope it's going to go well, you're nervous about what the future holds, you put your heart out there and hope that it doesn't get broken. There is a lot to think about and for someone who struggles with anxiety, every single worry is intensified. It's hard to explain how *terrified* an anxious person may feel about having their heart stomped all over. It is hard enough for the anxious individual to open themselves up to anyone, let alone make themselves vulnerable to love. The early stages of the relationship are by far the most anxious stages of all. There is so much uncertainty at this stage that the fears can easily feel too overwhelming when you don't have the right coping mechanisms to help you overcome relationship insecurity.

If you walked into a room full of people and ask them to put their hands up if they have ever felt nervous or anxious in a relationship, every single one of them would have their hands shooting up in the air. Even if it feels like no one understands your struggles with anxiety, it is important to remember that you are not the only one going through this. Relationships can be wonderful, filled with fun, laughter, joy, and lots of beautiful memories. But when there are issues in the relationship that need to be dealt with, like anxiety, for example, it can put a lot of strain and pressure between both people who are involved. One way of dealing with anxiety when it does arise in a relationship is to know what are the triggers that could cause an anxiety episode to happen. Although knowing the triggers is not actually solving the problem per se, when you can learn to recognize what might cause yours or your partner's anxiety to act up, you can take preventative measures to control the situation before it escalates out of control.

<u>Who Does Relationship Anxiety Affect?</u>

It can affect anyone who is looking for a loving and committed relationship and has experienced hurt in the past. Someone who might not necessarily have anxiety, in general, can develop relationship anxiety if the fear of being heartbroken again is strong enough to trigger that. As long as you are out there looking to find love, you could potentially be affected by relationship anxiety depending on the experiences you have had with love in the past.

Recognizing Your Relationship Anxiety Triggers

Here is a scenario for you to imagine. You've recently got to know this man or woman, and you've been chatting quite a bit over text. You've met up for a few coffee and dinner dates, and things were going really well. One morning, you decide to send him/her your usual good morning text the way you've been doing the last few weeks. Now, this person is having a very busy day. They've seen your text pop up on their phone, but decide to get back to you later because things are going crazy that morning with so much to do. Several hours pass, you keep checking your phone, feeling a little anxious that you haven't heard back from them yet. By late afternoon, there is still no text from them, and those unwelcomed, anxious thoughts are starting to flood your mind. Meanwhile, this person you've been seeing is still having a very busy day, and they have completely forgotten about responding to your text because they are so caught up in all the tasks they need to get done for the day.

After work, they head to the gym or an exercise class, do a quick grocery run, get home, cook dinner, and finally have a few moments to relax on the couch in front of the TV. Suddenly, they remember they forgot to reply to your text, and upon checking their phone, they have more than 20 missed calls from you and probably more than a dozen texts. Your anxious-self has text- bombed them throughout the day, and this person is completely taken aback, not sure what to make of all your missed calls and texts. They might even start backing off or feeling uncomfortable, thinking that you're coming on too strong and they're not ready for it yet. Meanwhile, you're fretting, anxious, and worried, wondering where it all went wrong and why they are pulling away from you. You regret calling multiple times and sending all those texts, but your anxiety-ridden brain couldn't help yourself. Does this sound familiar?

All you were trying to do is look for some reassurance that everything is all good, but instead, your actions have pushed the other person further away. If only you had better control over your anxiety and your actions, things might have worked out differently. This scenario example highlights why it is necessary to learn how to recognize your anxiety triggers. Nobody will know you better than you know yourself, not even your partner. You are the only one who can understand yourself completely, the only one who knows exactly what thoughts are running through your mind and what emotions are coursing through your veins at any given moment. To overcome your battle with relationship anxiety, it is imperative that you learn to recognize the anxiety triggers that cause a reaction within you. What is it that causes the anxiety to flare up when you could have been having a completely normal moment just a few minutes ago? While you will have the support of your loving partner, family, and friends to help you through those rough patches, it is important not to rely on them entirely either. They are there to help and support you, but *you need to help yourself first.* One day to do this is to learn how to recognize what triggers your anxiety.

Learning to recognize your anxiety triggers will help keep you calm during the early stages, in particular, when the relationship is still fragile. The early stages of the relationship are when couples are still trying to figure each other out. If you come off as too insecure, needy, and clingy from the very beginning, it might not be everyone's cup of tea. They want to be patient and be supportive, but when they are just starting to get to know you, they could be apprehensive and nervous too. They are just as worried about having their hearts broken by getting involved in a relationship that might not necessarily be right for them. Many relationships that had so much potential have fallen apart when anxiety took over, and if you don't want to change the relationship luck you have, recognizing your triggers is a step in the right direction.

When you have anxiety, you will try your best to avoid rejection and abandonment. This sometimes makes it difficult to navigate relationships (friendships included) when your partner might not understand your need for reassurance. Here are some anxiety triggers you can start learning to recognize:

• You Feel Suffocated - You want to be close to them and be around them all the time, but at the same time you feel suffocated, in a way. You struggle between your desire to be close to them and wanting to escape when everything feels like it is too much to bear. When you're dealing with anxiety, it can be difficult for you to open up to another person, even if you love them. You're afraid of being hurt and rejected. When you're around them, you feel happy until one or two of your fears start popping up and taking over your mind. These thoughts become all that you can obsess about and before you know it you feel suffocated and start looking for an escape path. Opening yourself up to another person in a relationship may cause your anxiety to trigger because you feel vulnerable, and on some level you believe that you are perhaps not worthy or deserving of their love. Anxiety can stop you from reaching the level of closeness that you desire that can be a very frustrating and stressful thing to deal with. You're afraid to open up to your partner and be intimate because you feel inadequate, believing that there is something "wrong" with you for feeling the way that you do, and you find it difficult to express your feelings of love, although you know that deep down inside, you do love them with all your heart.

• You Worry About Being Abandoned - You may try to squash it down and pretend like everything is okay, but deep down, you're always worried about being abandoned. You're always worried that your partner is going to get tired of putting up with your anxiety, pack their bags, turn around, and walk out the door for good. Since you already have a low opinion about yourself, this fear is going to feed into your anxiety about being rejected by your partner. The only thing you can think about are your flaws and you can't comprehend why your partner would want to be with someone like you. You end up worrying and obsessing possibly every waking moment that your partner is going to just reject you one day, especially because of your issues with anxiety. Whenever your partner is not able to be there for you because they're busy, you start to feel afraid that you are losing them or they are drifting away (even when you know the reason why they are busy). Living with anxiety is no easy task.

• The Fear of Being Hurt - You could be so terrified of getting hurt and putting yourself out there that anxiety begins to develop. The thought of being hurt can become so terrifying you shy away from the relationship before it has had a chance to blossom properly. You can't help but wonder where the relationship is going or if it has a chance, even when you know that you cannot predict the future. When you are dealing with anxiety, worrying about the future and knowing that nothing is guaranteed for certain is anxiety- provoking trigger that will probably plague you right from the beginning, and it can be difficult to deal with, especially when you don't know how to communicate those fears to your partner. Despite how much they reassure you they are not going anywhere, it doesn't do anything to alleviate your worries, and the anxiety still gnaws at you no matter how much you try to ignore it. Not all relationships work out, despite doing our best, but if we don't try at all, we could end up completely alone forever and this is not something that you want to deal with either.

• You're Worried the Relationship Is One-Sided - You worry that your partner might not love you as much as you love them. You worry that the relationship is one-sided, and as soon as your partner finds someone else, they will drop you without a second thought and you'll be left all alone. This feeds into your anxiety. When you're constantly replaying thoughts like this in your head on a loop, even the smallest thing can become a trigger for an emotional reaction. We might not want to admit it out loud, but we all worry about being alone. Humans are social creatures and we crave intimacy and a connection with other human beings, living in isolation has never been proven to work out well for anyone. Dealing with anxiety, you constantly worry about being alone. You worry that your anxiety makes people turn away from you, and they will not be able to love you for who you are because you've forgotten your own self-worth. You worry all the time and one of your worst fears is that the people that love you will eventually give up on you because your anxiety becomes too much for them to deal with.

●You're Jealous - You're jealous because deep down, you're terrified about losing your partner. Whenever you see them getting close to someone or giving them attention, your anxiety flares up. Thoughts start creeping into your head that you don't want to think about. *Is your partner cheating on you? Do they have feelings for that other person? Why are they so close?*

Should you be worried?

On the one hand, you know these thoughts are nothing more than a manifestation of your anxiety and probably hold no truth. On the other hand, you can't seem to stop yourself from becoming emotional and perhaps even hysterical because you are not in control of your thoughts. Each time you feel jealousy rising within you, stop and ask yourself if your partner really has given you any reason to be jealous? Where is this coming from? If they haven't done anything to make you jealous, why are you feeling this way? The only way to overcome this emotional trigger is to build up your confidence, which takes time. Learn to love yourself and know your worth, and slowly begin building your confidence from there.

● Feeling Like No One Understands You - Anxiety can be a very frustrating emotion to deal with, especially when you feel like nobody understands what you are going through. Nobody wants to deal with anxiety and the constant fear of losing the person that you love because of the issues that you are going through. Anxiety, when not dealt with properly, can have a severe impact on many aspects of your life, and even your partner's life because they are around you all the time. A relationship is an extremely precious thing because we all need love in our life.

Continue To Grow and Work on Yourself

Some truly intimate relationships involve some miscommunication, discord, or dispute. Though you tend to dwell on ways to avoid being neglected by your friend with tunnel vision to gain appreciation or love, you will certainly do everything you can to stop those issues. Chances are you will be sweeping your thoughts and desires under the rug. It is how you protect yourself. Over time, when you know precisely how alone you felt over your relationship, you will stumble over the ever-growing bump in the rug. You'll notice your wife's pain, and you'll even feel furious. It's a phenomenon that cannot keep you happy in the end. Luckily, there is a safer way out there.

By attentive self-awareness, you'll grow to support yourself, embrace the emotions, and be ready to confront insecurity.
You're likely to be more open to positive input from taking care of people in your life. As a result, you'll be able to interact more openly with your partner and listen to your partner's viewpoints

without being sidetracked by how they affect you. The result of this approach to coping with relationships is that you will be emotionally conscious and able to establish an emotional bond.

If you stay emotionally sensitive, caring, and articulate as conflict arises, you would be in a stronger position to maintain a healthy relationship. At the same time, you seek to resolve or cope with conflict.

This will take you through the dispute management process in just such a constructive manner.

Asking For Support.

The method of clearly expressing what you want allows you and your partner to concentrate on strengthening your relationship together.

Focusing on two principal activities could be helpful:

Share your thoughts, your expectations, and your wishes.

Tell what you want from your companion, clearly and concretely.

Types include:

As the husband Art goes out with his friends, Heather is angry. She generally

stews in her thoughts but doesn't share them with Art — which makes her feel more isolated from him and more anxious about missing him. Finally, she wants to tell him, "I feel lost when you go out with your friends and like I don't matter to you. I want you to have fun with the boys, but it's so hard for me." They're thinking about the issue, and he's saying he loves having time with his friends, so it's not a solution for her.

After some debate, they decide that he should also give her ample warning about his plans to make plans. He also promises that in the evenings when she winds up stuck at home, whether he's out or on his way home, he'll call or text her — just to let her know he's worried about her.

Sally often goes on work trips, leaving Max to feel depressed and doubt how much she truly cares about him. He has always helped her career, but he worries too much about her traveling, as he wants to spend time with her. He discusses this while making sure to stress that he encourages her to fulfill her desires.

While they do not come up with any answers to their differing needs, they believe they support each other. They reaffirm their engagement with the relationship and agree to talk and text daily when she is away, which helps.

Not all things do turn out that well, of course. When the discussions end poorly, make sure to go back to them when you're relaxed. Your objective is to find a way to feel cared about and relate to each other on an emotional level, even though you're struggling with a challenging problem. The following method will help you overcome some of those thorny problems.

Exercise: Starting A Difficult Conversation

The way you put your friend up to a question sets the tone of the discussion. Indeed, the Gottman Institute, which performs work related to marriage and partnerships, found that they could not only predict the outcome of a fifteen- minute discussion in the first three minutes but could also predict which spouses would split and which would stay married (Gottman and Silver, 1999; Carrere and Gottman, 1999). But think about how to launch a dialogue and observe the following guidelines:

Take a socially relaxed moment to converse. Timing isn't all that, but it is a number. If both parties are healthy enough to deal with it rationally and peacefully in the emotional and behavioral state, does a challenging discussion go well?

State the issue in brief. The only question is how it affects you, no matter what the friend has done or the situation. So quickly state the question and get to the real issue — how it affects you. Allow no liability. Moving on to all the negative stuff the friend has done or referring specifically to the character's flaws would make him defensive.

You're not going to get happier, and he's going to be more physically detached.

Concentrate on the experience. You just want him to understand and worry for you as much as you would want to lash out at or hide from your husband while he is bothering you. The only way he can do that is if you express your opinions and emotions freely.

One common way of doing so constructively is making assumptions about "I." If you initiate a statement with "I," you're saying something to your friend about what's going on with you — opening your life to him. In comparison, when you continue a sentence with "you," you're insulting your partner and stopping contact.

Imagine, for example, saying, "You rarely do something romantic anymore." This brings the point across, but you're far more likely to get the reaction you're hoping for by suggesting, "I wish you'd do anything sweet, like how you used to get me flowers for no reason." Or imagine that you and the husband spoke about his propensity to leave his dirty laundry on the floor, and he decided not to do something. You might say, "I feel frustrated with you for doing this. It builds me feel unloved and like I am your sweetheart. I'm just getting so sad." Compare that with saying,

"You're a slob and disrespectful. I don't know why I'm trying to talk about anything with you."

Need I Say More?

Of course, you can often use "I" statements to be insulting, such as, "I think you're an asshole." And, "you" statements can be emotional, such as, "You've tried to be helpful, but often I'm so angry that I can't take it in." So, when I'm dealing with people, I sometimes ask them to consider who they'd point out more when they're making the statement; this typically suits the person they're thinking about; the bottom line is that you want to open up about yourself and give your partner the chance to truly "see," support, encourage, and respect you.

Be explicit about your emotions. You may need to spend some time communicating your thoughts and identifying them. When you cannot do so, test the "Identify the Emotions."

Share this with your partner until you're sure about your thoughts. You may state, for example, "I feel depressed," or "I feel lonely." Say what your partner should do to meet your needs. He is strong. This also comes from expressing feelings. You might say, for example, "I feel unloved, and I need to know that you love me.

So if you squeezed my hand when we're out together or made

arrangements for us to spend time together, that would be nice." And you might say, "I feel sad and want us to be together. And I'd appreciate it if we were able to spend more time just relaxing and laughing about dinner." When you're unsure what your friend should do to make you feel comfortable, speak to each other about having a happier location solution.

Talking Through Conflicts

In addition to sharing your feelings and desires, healthy communication requires you to listen to and "get" your partner — not just understand your partner intellectually, but see situations through the eyes of your partner and empathize with her. You need to set your experience aside when doing so.

Don't break your friend off; as you clarify, the goal is to agree with you—no minimizing or denying your partner's feelings to protect yourself from the hurt elicited by those feelings. Furthermore, you don't have to compromise with your partner when you do so or give up on what you want. It's just that listening will take turns, you and your friend. Both of you must be open to communicating, "reading" one another, and interacting positively and respectfully. Using that approach, you will foster a sense of confidence, even in the most intimate and sensitive interactions.

Much like you have to be careful whether to launch a challenging debate, the strength of such a dialogue is not only in what you're talking about but in how you're doing it. This helps you be conscious, for example, that you do have prejudices and are fallible. Your willingness to see and accept this can encourage your openness to criticism, your sense of kindness, your willingness to apologize, and your capacity to forgive sincerely. Overall, to create a positive result, you must approach your partner to know him honestly or her and express your thoughts and emotions more vigorously. Instead, when you and your friend struggle to protect your viewpoints, you will find yourself trapped in different worlds or at odds.

Overcoming Obstacles

One of the biggest obstacles that occur in a relationship that is riddled with anxiety from either one (or sometimes both) partners is the worry about when your partner is going to pull the rug out from underneath you. The worry about when they are going to pack up and leave you is one of the common recurring themes when you're dealing with anxiety.

Overcoming the relationship obstacles that are caused by anxiety requires patience and love. Love from not just your partner, but love from yourself. You need to love yourself, or rather, learn to love yourself again because you are worth it, and anxiety has made you forget who you are and how much you are worth. Your partner chose to be with you, knowing that you have anxiety, and that means you are someone who is worth loving.

<u>Being In a Relationship When You Have Anxiety</u>
You have to take care of yourself. It is the best thing you can do. Anxiety is a mental illness, and no, it is not a bad thing. Everyone

has their own battles and demons to fight. Yours just happens to be anxiety. If you don't take care of yourself, you won't be able to exercise any of the other tips in this book that are designed to help you feel better. Taking care of yourself should be your number one priority. Despite what your anxiety will try to tell you, you *must* find a way to love yourself first before you can think about loving anyone else the way you believe they deserve. By loving yourself first, your relationship has a chance of survival. The love you share between you and your partner has to come from a loving, healthy, and stable foundation. If you don't have that stable foundation to fall back on, it becomes easy to let arguments and disagreements take control. Anxiety will convince you that there are a million problems and more in your relationship that you need to be worried about because that is what anxiety does best. When you don't have this stable foundation of love to work on, it can lead to obstacles like codependent and enabling behaviors. This can affect the relationships that you have in your life, and it isn't limited to romantic relationships alone either. You need to build that stable foundation of trust first by believing that you are someone who is worthy of love. Yes, you have a lot of anxiety issues that you are working through, but can you name anyone in this world who is perfect and without flaws? No, because such a person does not exist.

It Begins with A Mindset Shift

The problem that a lot of people who deal with anxiety go through is the fact that they tie their sense of self-worth to external factors. For example, you worry that your partner might leave you if you gain a little weight because you have tied your sense of self-worth to your appearance. Perhaps you believe your partner is going to leave you if you lose your job one day because you have tied your sense of self-worth to how much income you're making. Your sense of self-worth needs to come from within and to do that, you need to create a shift in your mindset before you work on overcoming your relationship obstacles.

• This Is Not a Competition - You're not in a competition with anyone and you don't need to put so much pressure on yourself to be perfect. Stop competing and stop comparing, it is only making your anxiety and insecurities a lot worse. You're competing because you're trying to determine where you stand in terms of your value, and that's the wrong mindset approach to take. You don't need to be as smart as your partner. You don't need to be as rich or earning as much as your partner. You don't need to be as well-dressed as your partner. You don't have to share all the same hobbies, likes, or dislikes as your partner. You are your own unique individual and so are they. None of those things matter. It is the way that you *complement* each other at the end of the day that makes the relationship strong. It is about what you can bring to the relationship and the love and support you have to offer someone else. Shift your mindset away from the notion of trying to be perfect to feel worthy of love. Your differences are what bring you together as a couple, and it is your difference that creates the glue that binds you together.

• Focus On the Good You Bring to The Relationship - The second mindset shift is to start moving away from all the "mistakes" and "flaws" anxiety will try to convince you that you have. To overcome anxiety for good, it is simply not enough to just change the way that you do things, but you must also change the way that you think and feel about yourself. In short, quit beating yourself up all the time thinking about all the ways in which you feel you are inadequate, and start seeing yourself in a positive light. Your partner CHOSE to be with you, and this means that you occupy a special place in their life. You have a special role to play that their friends and family don't, and it is time that you started embracing that. Your partner saw something that is special and unique in you, and they believed that they needed this part of you to fulfill what they were missing in their life. Focus on how wonderful that notion is. This step is going to be really hard in the beginning for a lot of people, but you must take this leap if you are serious about overcoming your anxiety. Anxiety has no room to grow if the space in your head is filled with positive thoughts. If you are finding this step difficult in the beginning, especially trying to come up with good things about yourself, seek help from your partner, family, and friends. Ask them to list one or two things that they love about you. You would be surprised to hear some of the responses, and things you may have viewed as flaws are actually what other people love about you the most.

● Focus On What Your Partner Needs - Instead of focusing on what you're lacking, shift your mindset, and start focusing on *what your partner needs* instead. Rather than allow your thoughts to be consumed by all the things you believe you lack, think about what your partner needs to become the best version of themselves. By shifting your focus to someone that you love, it gives you a purpose. Something to look forward to and something to live for. Focus on putting a smile on their face and focus on the sense of happiness you get knowing you were the reason behind why they feel happy. Depending on the severity of anxiety, sometimes having something different to focus on can make a big change in your life.

• Continue Working On Your Best Self - Working on becoming your best self is an ongoing process, but this is a great way to shift your mindset away from how anxious you feel. Again, it is about creating a different perspective and giving your mind something else to latch onto rather than the thoughts that make you worry. Anxiety will have you believe that you have nothing worthwhile or nothing of value to offer your partner, but that is where you're *wrong*. The best thing you can offer your partner is the very best version of yourself, even if that still happens to be a work in progress. Overcoming anxiety is going to mean that there are certain lifestyle choices, mostly bad habits in this case, that you are going to need to change, minimize or give up completely if you want to see a difference in your life for good. For example, your diet and the foods that you eat. It probably comes as no surprise that a poor diet can have a significant impact on our lives, and this includes causing certain diseases such as obesity, insomnia, low levels of energy, poor mental health, and yes, even anxiety. One thing that anxiety does is to cause us to feel poorly about ourselves. This explains why our self-esteem depletes so dramatically when we are dealing with anxiety. To boost your confidence once more and take control of your life again, you need to first start taking care of yourself. It is easier to feel better about yourself when you've done things that make you look and feel good, as opposed to doing nothing at all and feeling like you look like nothing but a big mess. Work on your energy, work on your health, work on your fitness, work on your happiness, keep working on yourself, and taking little steps forward in the right direction. Even if the change feels like it is tiny, if it makes a little difference in the way that you feel, that is more than good enough. If you're not already doing it, consider including exercise in your routine. Exercise is a great lifestyle choice that offers many benefits which most of the time won't cost you a penny. Exercises help to release endorphins which make you feel good, and working up a good sweat a few times a week will boost your mood in a significant way. Not only will you feel good about yourself, but you'll also start to look even better, which is great because it will help to boost your confidence, which is exactly what you need if you have anxiety.

- Keeping A Mood Journal - When your thoughts have nowhere else to go, turn to a mood journal. One of the problems that are faced by those who are dealing with anxiety is feeling too overwhelmed by their thoughts, worries, and fears. Yet, we're not brave enough to talk about some of these problems because we're still working through other anxious issues we might have, like the fear of being judged for our perceived "flaws." Keeping everything bottled up inside with no outlet to let it pour out is what makes it seem like it is difficult to cope and deal with. Hence, keeping a journal comes in handy in your quest to overcome anxiety and get rid of it from your life for good. It has an element of privacy that gives you a sense of security knowing that no one else is going to see this journal unless you want them to. A journal is something that is only for your eyes, and it provides you with a safe and private place where you can express every feeling and emotion you have without the fear of being ridiculed or judged. Expressing your emotions in a journal will not cause problems or conflict with anyone because it is only for your eyes. Your journal is also a place where you can record down the things that happened to you, especially the good things too, That way, you can look back on it later and remind yourself that you do have things to be happy about. When anxiety threatens to drown you out, let it all out and clear your mind by turning to your journal. When those thoughts are out of your head, it makes it much easier to regain some clarity.

<u>Obstacle Exercise #1: Accepting Your Past</u>

Everybody comes with a past, and if your current relationships are affected by the things that have happened to you in the past, it's because you haven't embraced your past. We come from different backgrounds, households, and have had relationships with different styles of communication. You might have grown up in a household that doesn't want to talk about their feelings all that much, or you might have come from a household that did a lot of shouting as a form of communication. You might have had relationships in the past that have left you hurt and scared. Either way, they are all a part of your past and they have contributed to the person that you are today. A lot of the trouble with anxiety stems from the fact that those who have it don't fully realize or comprehend what their behavior is doing to the people around them. They are not aware of how their anxious behavior is affecting the ones who are closest to them. If you want to overcome anxiety and get rid of it from your life for good, that needs to change.

Give yourself the time to process your past and slowly learn to accept it. It may not have been ideal, but nobody ever lives a perfect life. Everyone is doing the best that they can, and this includes you. There is always an issue to be worked through, and if it is not anxiety, it is going to be something else. You need to start paying more attention to the kind of thoughts that you have, be aware of what those thoughts are doing to you, and how the things that you think could be triggering or magnifying your anxiety. Take the time to work through this process before you commit to a new relationship. Otherwise, you'll always find history repeating itself as an obstacle that is difficult to overcome. The only way to learn to recognize the behaviors that are triggered by anxiety and the behaviors that are causing a problem in your relationship is to embrace your past and accept yourself for who you are. Everyone has qualities that they are not proud of but denying who you are and the past you came from is not going to make things any better. When you start paying more attention to the thoughts that are running through your head, actively stop yourself when you notice these thoughts are negative and immediately replace those thoughts with something positive instead. Instead of thinking that your partner doesn't really love you, remind yourself instead that your partner chose to be with you and how many times they have repeatedly told you that they love you.

Obstacle Exercise #2 - Taking Time to Enjoy Your Own Company

It can be scary to think about being left alone with our own thoughts, but you need to have this "me" time to yourself. It's the only way you are going to learn to love yourself. When you're dealing with anxiety, being alone may feel like the last thing in the world that you want to do. However, learning to

be alone is the thing you need to make you stronger. Think about alone time as a luxury, because it is becoming a rare thing these days. Work demands your attention. Responsibilities demand your attention. Family commitments demand your attention. Kids demand your attention. School demands your attention. You're being pulled in so many different directions you don't have time to pause and think about *your needs* anymore. The quality time that you get to spend with yourself could be spent getting to know yourself and your triggers better to aid in your recovery process.

We live in a world where we are constantly exposed to other

people and a lot of stimuli that could be a trigger for anxiety. In-person, over the phone, or online, we don't take enough time to enjoy our own company anymore. Spending quality time alone away from all the distractions in life has become a luxury, and this is now a luxury you should start utilizing more to help you overcome your relationship obstacles. While being in the company of others is not wrong, spending too much time around other people has made your anxious brain dependent on them. When they're not around, you feel lost and unsure of what to do with yourself, opening the door for your anxious thoughts to come flooding through. We have come to believe that we need to rely on other people to fill the missing pieces in our lives instead of relying on ourselves.

It is time to start taking baby steps and learn how to love your own company again. When you do, you gradually train your brain to be okay when you have no one else around you. You learn to become okay when your partner is busy and can't reply to your texts or phone calls right away. When you learn to enjoy your own company again, your brain doesn't automatically switch to panic mode and feel lost when you've got no one to turn to. Your mind becomes clearer, you listen to your intuition more, and you finally have time to reconnect to the things that you forgot you, love. The things that make you happy but forgot about it because you were too busy struggling with your anxiety.

<u>Obstacle Exercise #3 - Give Your Partner Time to Process Your Anxiety</u>

This might be the first time your partner has to deal with something like this. Before they fell in love with you and chose to be with you, they might not have dealt with something like this before. Relationship anxiety could be something new to them, and like you, they will need time to process everything that is happening. They might need time to educate themselves and you can help this process along by communicating with them as much as possible. Tell them what your symptoms are, let them know when you're not feeling okay and could use some extra support. Help them to recognize the signs and symptoms that you might need some extra help. Keep communicating with your partner about what your triggers are instead of trying to hide it. When both of you are aware of what could possibly trigger anxiety, you will be better equipped to take preventative measures to stop those triggers before they can do any damage. Have an open line of communication with them so they can better understand what you are going through. They may not understand right away, but they eventually will if the communication is ongoing and steady.

Be patient and work through this process together as a couple. A relationship is not a one-person job. It takes two people to make it work, and those two people need to work together as a team. Don't shut your partner out of the anxious part of your life. Part of overcoming relationship anxiety is working together because sometimes you are going to need support, especially when there are moments that you feel you don't have the strength to do this alone. When your partner tries to make attempts to be there for you, let them. Show them how grateful you are for their help. There is only so much you can do on your own, sometimes we could all use a helping hand, even if we are not dealing with anxiety. You need to rely on each other, love each other, support each other the best way you can, and above all else, accept each other for who you are. Be honest with your partner about how they can help. Let them know what you need from them to help you overcome anxiety and what they can do to make you feel better. If they know specifically what works and what doesn't, they'll be able to better help you through the recovery process. Let them know what you are thinking and what is bothering you if you need someone to talk to. Don't expect your partner to change according to how you want them to be, and likewise, they shouldn't expect the same from you either.

<u>Obstacle Exercise #4 - Breathe, and Do It Mindfully</u>

If the everyday stimuli you are exposed to is putting your fight or flight response in a constant state of stress, it's time to slow down and breathe. Breathe, and do it mindfully. It is a tool that you can tap into every single day, and it is one of the most naturally calming tools you have at your disposal. Since breathing happens so automatically for us, we don't give much thought to how it can help when we're dealing with anxiety. Mindful breathing is a useful exercise to have on hand because when faced with anxiety, you tend to lose control of your breathing and that is why you start experiencing chest pains and difficulty catching your breath. When you are under stress, your breathing becomes shallower and more ragged, which when combined with anxiety, can lead to panic attacks and hyperventilation.

Before, during, or after a stressful event or encounter, breathe. Breathe mindfully and do it as long as you need until you physically feel your heart start to slow and return to its normal pace. It's hard to see how sitting in silence, even if it is for five minutes, focusing on your breath is going to make a difference.

Try this exercise right now. Whether you're sitting or standing, reading this, get comfortable for a minute. Adjust until you find a comfortable position, allow yourself to settle. Now, let your eyes softly close, and tune in to your entire body. Feel your shoulders relax, feel your muscles relax as you make a conscious effort to do so.

Turn your attention to your breath, focus on how the air goes in as you inhale, and out again as you exhale. With each exhale, allow yourself permission to let go. With each exhale, imagine one anxious thought gradually leaving your body. Focus on how your body feels, how your hands, spine, back, legs, feet, everything. Focus on purposely relaxing all your muscles as you exhale the breath from your body. Allow yourself to let go of expectations and judgments. Focus on breathing to help calm and relax you whenever you are faced with an anxiety episode. Become aware of the air that is flowing in and out of your body. Inhale through your nose, and exhale slowly. Breathe in for four counts slowly, relax, and then exhale slowly with the same count. Whenever you feel your anxiety rising, immediately switch your focus to your breathing and practice those techniques until you feel yourself calming down again.

With each breath, remind yourself that you are good enough.

Remind yourself that anxiety does not control you as you feel your heart start to slow down and return to its normal pace. Remind yourself that you are the one in control of your mind, body, and soul, and this breathing technique is proof of that. Notice that by not doing anything other than bringing awareness to your breath, your body is beginning to relax in a natural way without being forced.

Obstacle Exercise #5 - Work Together As A Couple

Working together as a couple means learning to do activities that you both enjoy and using that time to form a closer bond. Everyone gives and receives love in different ways. A small gesture could be the most meaningful thing in the world for some people. Anxiety can cause a couple to be so wrapped up in all their worries and fears that they forget a relationship is supposed to be about enjoying yourself with your partner. It's easy to forget about enjoying the little things in life and the small gestures when all you can think about are your fears. It's easy to forget to be happy. To alleviate your fears, you need to have fun together, enjoying each other's company. As part of the process of overcoming anxiety, you need to remember what it was like to have fun again as a couple. When you're having fun, it is hard to feel worried and fearful, especially when it is an activity that you love and you're lost in the moment.

Nothing beats spending quality time together. Having fun together as a couple is an excellent distraction technique. For it to work effectively, pick activities that both of you enjoy doing together as a couple, not just an activity that one person is going to enjoy. Both of you need to equally have fun because that is how you bond, and you're going to need to do a lot of bonding and healing to recover from the strain that anxiety has caused. You don't have to do anything extra special or expensive, and you don't need to plan outrageous vacations together if you don't feel like it. The simple act of setting aside maybe an hour a day to focus entirely on your partner alone is enough to make it special. When you're dealing with anxiety, knowing that this person is taking time out of their day to focus on nothing but you, that is saying something. Other things you could do together as a couple include going for an outdoor hike or a walk in the park on a beautiful, sunny day. Maybe watch a movie together on the couch and laugh at the funny moments. Cook together, play board games, read, play music around the house, laugh, share, talk. It could be anything that brings you and your partner close together and for that one hour (or however long you choose to spend), anxiety is a distant memory.

If your partner is the one struggling with anxiety, know that this time you spend with them means the world to them. It is the kind of support they need from you, and a gesture like this is more meaningful than all the expensive gifts in the world. You being more than you will ever know, especially if separation anxiety is one of their triggers. Having you around them and supporting them will make a difference. When they are around the people that they love, especially if they are doing fun activities together, it makes it is harder to focus on anxieties. When you are around your partner and you notice that an anxiety episode may be looming, try suggesting a fun activity that the two of you can do together to quickly distract them and get their mind off things. The more time you spend with your partner, the better you will make them feel because eventually, they will start to realize as they slowly overcome anxiety, that you really do love them and genuinely want to spend time being around them. This helps them feel a lot better about themselves, which will help with their recovery process. The best gift that you can give them is the gift of love.

Feel Proud of How Far You've Come

Anxiety is an uphill battle, and you should feel proud that you have made it this far when it has no doubt been hard for you. You are going through a lot, and overcoming anxiety sometimes may seem impossible to them. Feel proud of how far you've come if you've made it this far, and encourage your partner to remind you of how much progress you've made too when you forget.

Anxiety And Panic Attacks

Anxiety can effectively lead to panic and anxiety attacks, which is nothing new. But you need to remember that while conflicts occur, it is for your good that you keep calm if you have problems with panic and anxiety. Such situations can easily trigger an attack, which can make everything go worse. Anxiety and panic attacks are generally characterized by:

- Sweating
- Difficulty breathing
- Difficulty concentrating
- A feeling of unknown doom
- Racing thoughts

Although there is nothing new to say, these symptoms are not funny. So, you need to be mindful before getting into an argument that if you fail to be level headed, you might face an attack.

Being Defensive

Nothing can be more destructive to the constructive resolution of conflicts than the habit of defensiveness. Anxiety can effectively block out the rational portion of your mind that plays the part of thinking about a situation with logic. When this logic is not present, you might face a tough time in focusing on what is being said by your partner. You are most likely to shift your focus from listening to lashing out. You will turn out the defensive shield, even in situations when your partner is not attacking you. You should defend your position when you are being treated unjustly. However, if your partner is willing to opt for a peaceful resolution of the issues, the best action is to match their intentions. You will need to drop your defensive shield for the betterment of the relationship. But when you are having anxious thoughts, doing all these is not going to be easy.

Shut Down

In place of just turning on your defensive mode, you might choose to shut down completely. Your anxious mind might find it tough to process all those things that are happening. The lack of energy during the situation can lead to a complete shutdown. As such a thing happens, you will not be able to concentrate or focus. You will not be able to call out rationality or logic for working through the conflict. Also, you will not be able to comprehend what is being said by your partner. You will be feeling empty and heavy on the inside, feeling like a battery that has drained suddenly. The best thing that can be done on your side in such a situation is to relax and mend. Conflicts will be in place unless you can take back control over your mind and activate rationality.

<u>How To Successfully Overcome a Bad Relationship Dispute?</u>
When you face a conflict in your healthy and growing relationship, try to think about how you can talk or express your feelings regarding this conflict.

The primary aim is to establish a good communication model. Good communication is where every individual can check the stock and get an idea about the other person's attitude. The conflict resolution will seem a lot easier to manage when it is not escalated with unnecessary things such as angry tones. For effective communication during conflicts, you will need to follow three simple rules:

Keep your calm, and do not raise your voice.

Let your partner talk. Let them develop the state of the

argument, as communication not only includes talking but listening also.

Try to reach a middle ground; however, do not opt for compromises that can negatively affect the coming days.

A couple who has the habit of arguing and respects all these rules can quickly resolve.

Required Actions for Overcoming Conflicts Between Partners

Relationships are not meant to be easy. You will keep learning when you are in a healthy relationship. Is it even possible to not repeat the mistakes and stabilize the base of your romantic relationship? Is it possible to manage the relationship conflicts without you being hurt? Try to follow all these recommendations for rebuilding the love in your struggling relationship.

After you are well aware of the reasons behind the relationship tensions that tend to shake the relationship base, you can focus on moving to a more 'direct' phase of harmony. Yes, the first phase might turn out to be very psychological, as you will need to communicate with the other person. However, it is necessary if you want to bring back your relationship on its track.

It is essential to use more thoughtful and technical actions to find your partner's heart. It is also needed to overcome the relationship crisis.

The actions that you decide upon to use needs to correspond with various issues. Otherwise, your actions will not have any kind of effect on the situation. It can even aggravate the issues. Do not just opt for resolution for the sake of being done with it; opt for resolution for making the situations better.

Do not keep assigning blame to the other side. A relationship is not a one-person game. It is all about team effort. Both partners are required to be in the relationship altogether. If one of the partners keeps on giving effort while the other just sits idle, it will be better for the relationship to exist.

If you or your partner is not feeling satisfied or fulfilled in your relationship, you must spend more time together. It will help you both to understand the problems in a better way. You will also come to know what you both want and need from the relationship.

Every relationship in this world is bound to go through conflicts at some point or the other. All that is important for you to know is that disagreements are not always a bad thing. It is how individuals in relationships try to express their varying views on a topic or situation.

<u>Compromising As a Common Solution</u>

The use of compromise in relationships is widespread for resolving disputes and disagreements in the mediation and negotiation process. While it can lead to an agreement's production, compromise is not powerful enough for resolving conflicts all the time. It cannot work specifically in situations when there are some underlying organizational or interpersonal conflicts. The prime reason for this is that compromise is a settled resolution to an issue. It is not at all the ultimate solution which is sought by either partner. It can effectively generate material or a functional solution. But it cannot resolve behavioral or emotional issues that are coupled with disagreements. As a result, either one of the partners or both will continue to carry forward certain ill feelings or dissatisfaction that might come to the surface once again if the issue arises.

Compromise is being defined as a win/lose agreement where both the partners tend to get something of what they wish for. But it is not possible to attain everything that they want. The majority of the tensions or issues crop up with a collaborative or competitive strategy. The outcome that is best possible in such a situation is the ultimate goal of both partners. But various other vital factors come into the equation, such as financial cost, time requirement, practical matters, and use of power. The ultimate realization that the desired outcomes might turn out to be unachievable can force the partners to negotiate. It involves the concept of giving and take for reaching a mutual agreement of compromised nature.

<u>Agreeing To Disagree</u>

Using a compromise for settling a dispute or conflict requires both the partners to be aware that the result might be less than they hoped for. The ultimate decision might be the one that is acceptable, however, not optimal. You may feel resistance or reluctance to compromise to resolve conflicts when you think the result will be lost. When the primary focus is on things that are achieved, instead of things that have been given up, chances of acceptance and satisfaction of both partners is high. Compromise will turn out to be a successful venture if both partners have a choice of tangible outcomes. The outcomes are required to be open for consideration so that the final decision always remains within a standard box for both partners.

There might be a requirement to 'agree to disagree' at some point in cases when the issues seem incurable and the realization that they will be unable to agree to sets in. Agreeing to disagree is essential when the disagreement is over principles or values rather than methods or facts. When both partners can learn to listen to each other and respectfully understand the other person's point, accepting the disagreements will seem a lot easier. A mutual form of acceptance regarding the differences can improve the likelihood of a proper resolution to any issue or dispute.

Compromise can turn out to be a perfect and effective method for resolving differences and conflicts. However, it might not be the right choice all the time. Opting for compromise, even when other modes of conflict seem more appropriate, can lead to an outcome that is of no use for the current situation. You will need to make sure that essential requirements or vital issues are not lost during compromise. Sometimes you might need to opt for other creative solutions. All forms of disagreements and differences are not needed to be negotiated.

Meditation For Anxiety

The goal of anxiety and stress relief meditation is to learn how to let go of whatever weighs you down and realize the peace and calmness the mind can experience. It serves the purpose of helping someone understand the position they are now in. The past and the future are impermanent. By letting these thoughts cloud our judgment and state of mind, we accept the troubles they drag along with them.

When it comes to anxiety and stress relief, it is highly advisable to separate yourself from everyone else. You need time to restore yourself to your most productive element because you might rub off some of the bad energy onto others. If need be, hide in an adequately ventilated closet for as long as you are comfortable. Close your eyes and try to relax your body. This is important to prepare it to get into a state of wellbeing. Focus your attention on yourself. This is your time; forget all the other things that cloud your mind. You want to be at peace and resonate peace, and this is your time to manifest its existence. Start by inhaling and exhaling slowly through the nose and mouth in that order.

Observe your body and the buildup of tension accumulated from the anxiety and stress.

You can imagine a stream of river passing and washing away all the buildup of anxiety and stress. Let it all go; let it all wash away. You can imagine anything. You can also decide to fold your stress and anxiety in a leaf and let it go in whichever direction the wind decides. Every time you exhale, envision all the worries go away. Your mind is your palace of imagination.

You can do anything in the space you have created for yourself now.

Slowly, go back and observe your breathing again. Keep inhaling through your nose and exhaling through the mouth. You can decide to let it happen naturally or give it intervals of three seconds. Your space your choice. If your mind keeps wandering, you can perform a couple of deep breaths to bring back your focus to your breathing.

Now, imagine you are all alone at the beach, and you have worn your favorite pair of swimsuits. You want to take a dip because you are aware of the calming effect water has on you. Picture yourself running towards the water and splashing your way in. To your surprise, when you take a dip, you start to glow and feel so lovely. The more you dip yourself into the water, the more your worries wash away, leaving you with a pleasant aura and a sense of peace. Keep imagining this before going back to observe your breathing.

Notice if there is any change in your breathing. Does it feel more natural and relaxed? Do you feel better? If not, start with the breathing again. Center yourself and your thoughts. Do not let your source of stress or anxiety plague you in this space. Remember, this is your personal space. This is your time. Nobody can take away your time.

You can use any relevant scenario as a visual tool to let go of the stress and anxiety that had manifested itself. It does not have to be precisely what is given above. If it works for you, that is all that matters. Keep transitioning from your breathing to visual scenarios till the time you desire. Even after feeling better, you might decide to continue doing it for a while just because you can. There is certainly no harm in that.

Apart from the above method, mindfulness meditation, some audio guided meditations, and Vipassana meditation perform as suitable alternatives to try. The practice of meditation does not restrict you from trying out something different if the one you are accustomed to doing does not show results. Any technique that is good for you is the best.

A Deep Breathing Exercise

When practicing the following deep breathing exercise, you need to be in a quiet environment before you move on to the steps:

Begin by sitting upright in a chair or on the floor in any comfortable position, such as on your back.

Keep your eyes shut to reflect inward and focus.

Begin to be aware of your breath. Are you breathing slowly or very fast?

Now begin to breathe intentionally, making sure to keep your shoulders relaxed and still. Inhale deeply and slowly through your nose. You will feel your diaphragm expand as you can fill your body with air. Now you can begin to slowly exhale through your mouth, allowing the stale air to leave your body.

Continue to focus on your breath; repeat 5-10 more cycles of deep breathing.

The moment you begin to breathe deeply, you will notice that some areas of your body feel less tense than other areas. This is because your body releases stress with each exhale.

Before you conclude this exercise, notice how you feel physically, mentally, and emotionally.

To get the most out of this exercise, you must practice regularly, and at times, you do not even feel anxious.

Another strategy to help you cope with anxiety is progressive muscle relaxation. This is an exercise that you can use to reduce disturbing bouts of anxiety. It is a type of relaxation technique, and it can help you in moments of high stress or during a panic attack. By relaxing your body, you will be able to let go of anxious thoughts and feelings.

Creating A Sense of Security in Relationships

Relationships are unpredictable. You can't control everything and have it your way a hundred percent of the time. If you're someone who struggles with anxiety, how do you get the security that you need *despite* the unpredictability? If you want to feel secure in your relationship, you need to *create* that sense of security yourself. It is not going to magically happen overnight, and it is not going to be an instant fix either.

 A Secure Relationship Begins With *YOU*

If you're always going to rely on other people to make you feel secure, you are never going to feel *truly* secure no matter what relationship you find yourself in. There will always be a reason to feel anxious whether it's your friendships, relationships with your family, romantic relationships, and professional relationships too. In a romantic relationship, your partner could reassure you a thousand times that you are beautiful, smart, funny, handsome, good looking, perfect for them in every way, but none of that is going to make any difference if *you don't believe in it first.* Yes, anxiety can make it difficult to hold on to your confidence and self-esteem, but that does not mean it is impossible.

Security begins from within, and it starts by getting to know yourself inside and out. You need to be crystal clear about what you want, what you don't want, what you like, dislike, what your boundaries are, how much you're willing to put up with, what you look for in a partner, friend, family member, and more. You need to be clear about the things you want and start building a sense of confidence from there. Insecurities and negative self-talk are linked together, and one will always exist in the presence of the other.

Overcoming your insecurity only seems like an impossible challenge because your anxiety is convincing you right now that it cannot be done. *But it can be done,* and these are the steps you need to work through one at a time:

● Make A List and Cross It Off One by One - You will probably have several things you feel insecure about, and what you need to do is make a list of all your insecurities. This list will give you a clear idea of what you're working to overcome, rather than have it all up in your mind, jumbled together with all your other thoughts. There is something about writing things down on paper that creates a sense of clarity, and once you have a list of insecurities you feel are holding you back, work on them one at a time. The important point to remember is to work through these one at a time because as tempted as you are to knock off all your insecurities at once, slow and steady is the best approach to take. If you try to do too much too soon, you're going to overwhelm your anxious nerves. On your paper, pick one insecurity from the list to work on first. Next, ask yourself where this insecurity is coming from and what the root cause of it is. Don't avoid your insecurities, embrace them. Cry about them if you have to, but don't deny or reject them anymore. Most people try to push down their insecurities because they don't want to feel the way that they do. For the anxious individual, the idea of confronting these insecurities is even more alarming.

● Ask Yourself If You Are Willing to Change - Next comes the mindset shift. Once you've identified the insecurities you would like to work through, the other important question you need to ask yourself is whether you are willing to change. Are you willing to see things differently? To change your perspective? Sometimes, all it takes is a little tweak in perspective to make us see things in a different light, even with the anxiety. The key is to be open and willing to change. You need to let go of any mental resistance that could be holding you back. Be willing to create that shift in perspective because you know you deserve it. You know that you owe it to yourself to create a better, happier, frame of mind for yourself. Take another piece of paper and write down what it would look like if you treated yourself with love. If you're quick to treat your partner with love, how would it look like if you now did the same thing for yourself? Instead of thinking of yourself as a victim of your anxious thoughts, start looking at yourself through the eyes of love. Imagine if you saw a loved one struggling with the same anxious thought you had. You would immediately grab them, give them a big hug, and tell them they are good enough just the way that they are. It's about time you started treating yourself with the same kind of love you shower upon others.

● Focus on Thoughts That Support You - When dealing with anxiety, you will hear a lot of talk about reprogramming your mindset. There is a reason for that, and that reason is since anxiety begins in the mind, the mind is the one place we start working on to conquer the problem. If anxiety can make you think one negative thought, then you can train your brain to think about a positive thought that counteracts the negative one. Thoughts that empower you and support this new version of yourself that you are trying to create should serve as a reminder to yourself that you're good enough the way you are, and you deserve to have good things happen to you too. If you can tell the people you love how amazing and incredible they are and how deserving they are of love, why not do the same for yourself? For happiness to exist long-term, self-love needs to be present. Insecure thoughts do nothing but pull and weigh you down, and for every negative, there is a positive. It is time to start focusing on the positive thoughts to offset what your anxiety is trying to have you believe. Turn to the good old pen and paper again and write down the thoughts you have that make you insecure, cross them out with a big, bold, line, and write an empowering thought instead. For example, if your insecure thought is *I am not good enough for my partner*, you would cross that out and replace it with I have so much love

to give and my love makes the relationship stronger.

Refute your negative thoughts by writing a new

supporting thought in its place.

• Use Repetition - Once you're down writing all the empowering thoughts that make you feel supported, you're going to find that what you're left with is a list of positive affirmations. The next thing you want to do is repeat these affirmations to yourself over and over again until they become ingrained in your mind. Positive affirmations are what can be used to replace the negative thoughts that dwell within your mind causing you the social anxiety that you don't want to have. Part of challenging yourself to change and to gradually rebuild your self-confidence is to simply follow the same method that happens when you have a negative thought stemming from anxiety. Instead of allowing the negative thought to overcome your mind, use a positive affirmation as a thought replacement instead. Repetition is the key to making it stick.

• Stop Comparing Yourself to Others - Another shift in mindset you need to create is to stop comparing yourself to other people. Comparing has never been beneficial for anyone. This shouldn't be a competition, and the mindset that we should be adopting instead is that we are all in this together. We should spread love and focus on helping each other rather than tear each other down. Comparison is a destructive habit and it will do nothing to help the successful mindset you're trying to build. You're unique and you have the potential to reach your own kind of success. There is no point in comparing yourself to someone else because the truth is, you're never going to be that person. You're as unique as your thumbprint is. No two people are alike the same way no two sets of thumbprints will ever be alike. It's how we distinguish ourselves from the rest. To become more confident, that little pernicious voice in your mind must be silenced. Your inner critic does nothing but complains, put your down, and sow needs of negativity and doubt in your mind. You don't need all of that in your life, it is not going to benefit you in any way. Put a stop to the comparison and you'll find that you're much happier when you do. You have to find a way to stop worrying about losing your partner to someone you *think* is better than you. Your partner chose to be by your side, and that is something you should always think about. They didn't choose anyone else, they chose you, and that action should speak louder than words. Every person on this earth has their own life experiences and stories, and there is *no way* to compare one person to the person next to them. If you have to compare, compare yourself to the person you were six months ago, a year ago, or five years ago. It is progress, not perfection, that matters at the end of the day. Find the light that you have within and let it shine through.

● Catch Yourself When You Notice Your Mind Drifting Toward Negativity - When you catch yourself having an insecure or negative thought, put a stop to it by reminding yourself of your strengths. Be *proud* of your strengths. A positive state of mind will always win out at the end of the day. It may require a lot more work since negativity has a stronger influence, but it always wins. Always. Our brains are naturally wired for negativity, and it takes the brain four times longer to store good things than bad. We search for flaws before we focus on strengths, and we prefer to criticize before we complement them. We're instinctively drawn to negativity and we don't treat ourselves any differently. Your confidence lies in your ability to pay attention to your talents, your strengths, your achievements, and the advantages you have to offer. Commit time each day to remind yourself of your strengths to start boosting your confidence. Program your mind to only focus on your strengths. This is going to take a while, but it can be done, even if you are dealing with anxiety. You always have the ability to control your mind, and that is something a lot of people tend to forget. We let our minds and our thoughts get the best of us when we are the ones who are actually in control. Stay consciously active and pay attention to the thoughts that drift in and out of your mind throughout the day. Once you notice they're starting to slip toward the negative, pull them back straight away by focusing on the strengths you have and everything about yourself that you should feel proud of.

Communication Is the Key

People cannot read your mind or your body language. To you, the hints and signs may be clear, but to them, they might not realize there is a problem at all. Communicating effectively in a relationship that doesn't have to deal with anxiety is challenging enough. When you bring anxiety into the mix, it gets even more complicated. This part of the process is something you are going to have to work on together with your partner. It takes two people to improve communication in a relationship, especially when that relationship has to deal with anxiety. Healthy communication in a relationship is about both partners listening to each other and expressing themselves in
the most effective way. Both partners need to be
doing their part to make the communication process successful.

When dealing with anxiety, the partner who is going through the anxiety will sometimes struggle to make themselves understood. It can be hard to explain the reason behind their fears, and sometimes you might struggle to find the words to do so. For the partner who has to deal with their anxious partner, it can be an equally stressful process. Sometimes it feels as if the situation is not fair to you. When you signed up for this relationship, this wasn't what you had in mind. A partner's anxiety can have a major impact on your life, even though you are not the one with anxiety. Your life suddenly seems to be powerless because you see the person that you love spiral out of control so often and you have no idea what you can do to help. Nothing you seem to do ever seems to be enough. It is also normal to experience sadness over the situation because this relationship was not what you had in mind. You love your partner regardless, but because the relationship is plagued with anxiety, it is not exactly the life that you envisioned for yourself and your partner. That is completely understandable. When we enter into a relationship, most of us already have an idea or a picture in our heads about what a happy relationship would be like. Anxiety was never in the picture so it is understandable to feel sad when the reality is not quite what you thought it would be.

To overcome anxiety battles, communication is the key. However, you must first understand that approaching this situation is going to be a challenge. This isn't going to be a quick fix, like fixing a broken sink in your kitchen. Overcoming relationship anxiety is a long-term process that, unfortunately, comes with no quick fix and overnight solution methods. Ideally, you and your partner should work together as much as possible, although that can be difficult especially in the early stages because anxiety prevents them from looking at situations rationally without overreacting. When your partner is dealing with anxiety, they are constantly worried and fearful. These are the two primary emotions that they are feeling. This constant state of worry and fear makes them less aware and unable to tune in to the needs of their partner because they are unable to focus on anything except their own worries and fears. When they are in this state, they find it difficult to trust and connect with anyone, even their partners. They may even feel that you are not being there for them in the way that they need because they are not thinking clearly. Without communication, it can be almost impossible to understand each other, let alone work together as a team.

To improve your communication as a couple that has to deal with anxiety, this is what you need to do:

• Listen to Understand Rather Than Respond - Most people seem to "listen," when really what they are doing is waiting for you to finish your statement so they can jump in with their point of view. That is not the qualities that embody good communication. There's a very big difference between listening and listening actively. You could be listening and nodding along, saying all the right things, but your mind is actually a million miles away or thinking about something else. That's not active listening. It can be extremely annoying and frustrating for both partners to feel like they are never being heard. How can you help each other work through the anxiety if no one is actually listening to the *real cause* of that anxiety? Active listening is when you take in everything that your partner is saving, process it, and stay engaged throughout the entire conversation. You know exactly what to say when to say it, and how to say it because you have been paying attention. That is active listening. Do your best to understand each other and see where the other person is coming from. When your partner is going through an anxious moment, do your best to approach the situation calmly so you can help them to calm down. Do not react equally emotionally, because that could just escalate the situation when they are already in a highly emotional state of mind. You need to remain calm and steady before attempting to calm your partner down. Encourage them to talk to you about what they are feeling. If they don't want to share, don't push them, give them their space but keep reminding them you are there if they need to talk. Don't walk away from them, leave the room, or turn away from them because that would just trigger their fear of abandonment and rejection. Put yourself in your partner's situation. When you learn to actively listen to each other, it makes for a much better conversation. It also brings you one step closer to better understanding the anxiety triggers and how to overcome them should they pop up next time.

● Avoid Being Critical - When you communicate with each other, both partners might be experiencing a sense of frustration. The anxious partner might feel frustrated they are not being understood, while the other partner feels frustrated because their efforts to calm their anxious partner seem to be falling on deaf ears. In that frustration, try your best to avoid being critical of your partner. When you're listening to them, try to do it with empathy. Ideally, you want to let your partner be the one who is doing all the talking. It is their time to talk. However, if they were to ask what you think or what you would suggest at some points during the conversation, then your job here is to not respond critically or judgmentally. Listening with empathy is one step up from listening actively. It is about making your partner feel supported, about letting them know that you can see things from their perspective, and you understand why they feel the way that they do. A partner with anxiety may sometimes have trouble expressing how they really feel. They may try to suppress their emotions because they are worried about driving you away, but suppressing their emotions only makes the anxiety much worse. The more that they try to reject and suppress their emotions, the worse their anxiety may become and it could even end up spiraling out of control. As a result, they could be prone to irrational behavior and become defensive as a way to protect themselves from their fear of being hurt. Don't ridicule, judge, or criticize them for their opinions because remember, it is all about them this time. The best thing for you to do in this situation would be to approach your partner with kindness and empathy. Remind them that you are not going anywhere, and if they need someone to talk to, encourage them to trust you enough to open up. This may take some time though and a lot of persuasions, so you are going to need to exercise a fair amount of patience here to help them through the process.

• Stay Focused on Solutions Instead of Problems - When poor communication happens, it is because the two people involved are focusing on the problems instead of the solutions. Admittedly, it can be hard to ignore the very obvious problem of your partner's anxiety, but instead of focusing on everything that is going wrong, why not try a better approach? Focus on the solutions instead and see what a difference that makes to the way you communicate. What is a solution instead that is going to work best for both of you? Having a focused conversation with your partner during their moments of anxiety can be difficult because it is easy to get sidetracked and the topic could easily wander off into unrelated territory. This is why you need to stay focused on the subject of discussion at hand and not let the conversation get out of control. When talking to your partner, steer the conversation back in the right direction whenever it threatens to veer off course. Always stay on point and do not let yourself get carried away by your partner's emotions because it will not solve the problem at hand which you started off discussing in the first place. Stay calm during the conversation and use positive reinforcement sentences. For example, you can thank them for bringing the problem to your attention and then talk about how to work through this together as a team.

• Be Focused for Your Partner - If your partner's anxiety won't let them stay focused, you can do it for them. Being in a relationship with someone who is dealing with anxiety can only mean one thing. You are the rational, level-headed one in the relationship. Therefore, you need to be the voice of reason in the relationship until your partner has had a chance to calm down again. You are the one that can think straight and you are the one that is able to communicate more effectively. You, in essence, are the one who is more in control. When you communicate with your partner, you need to be specific and make clear what it is that you want from them. You need to be their guiding light in this scenario, and if there is something you need from them or want them to do, you need to make it clear. Be specific when you communicate with them. Be clear when you're communicating with each other.

• Turn Off the Distractions - The biggest distraction being your mobile phone. To avoid the main points of your conversation being lost in translation, finding a good place where you can communicate effectively is going to be your best bet. For example, you could try looking for a quieter place in the house to sit down and talk, a place where the distractions are kept to a minimum. There is nothing worse than opening your heart to someone and trying to tell them how you feel, only to be interrupted by the constant buzzing and beeping of their mobile phones. Another way to minimize distraction is to turn off mobile devices (one of the main causes of distraction today, especially among the millennials). Remove the source of the distraction. Relevant and important information is in danger of being missed if you are not able to listen without being distracted by what your partner is trying to say to you. You really need to be able to listen and listen *well* if you hope to improve your communication skills moving forward. The fewer distractions you have, the higher the chances of improved concentration and focus when a discussion is taking place, thereby improving effective communication.

• Using the Right Words - When communicating with each other, use the word *"I"* to express how you feel. Word selection is important in determining how effectively your messages come across. Words are the source of facilitating effective communication, and careless or improper use of words is usually the reason for poor communication. With an anxious partner, it is important that you pay attention to your choice of words more than ever. In an effort to improve the effectiveness of your communication, start by carefully considering the types of words used in delivering your message. What you can do, instead, is to opt for common and familiar words, single words that deliver the point across more concisely instead of several words, use shorter words where possible instead of longer phrases. In your partner's anxious and panicked state, they are unlikely to be able to think rationally. Complicated sentences will be lost on them. The more concise and succinct your messages, the easier it is to understand.

• When They Talk, Let Them Talk Without Interrupting - This works both ways. When your partner is talking to you, it is important to let them finish and avoid jumping in or butting in half when they are in the middle of saying something. Let them finish what they were trying to tell you. The more you interrupt them, the more frustrated and anxious they are going to become. When they are talking, what you can do as a supportive partner is to show empathy. Being empathetic to your partner means letting your partner know that you can understand what they are going through. It means letting your partner know that you are genuinely concerned about them. The best way to be empathetic towards your partner is to put yourself in their shoes and see the world the way they are seeing it. Being empathetic with your partner means letting them know and communicating with them as often as possible that yes, you can understand why they feel the way that they do. Although you may not agree with what they are thinking or saying, you need to be patient with them and remind yourself that they are only behaving this way because of their anxiety, and this is what you need to do as a supportive partner to help them overcome this hurdle. Compassion is the best way to deal with this. It may be frustrating for both partners to deal with anxiety but try to picture yourself in each other's shoes again. Imagine being plagued by worry all the time and spending your waking hours afraid something bad could happen at any moment. Imagine living in a state of always worrying about losing the one that you love. Think about how that would make you feel. It can't be easy living in fear like that. Don't become impatient and angry with them over their selfish behavior, instead be as compassionate as you can. Show them that they have nothing to worry about and sympathize with them. If you are the one dealing with anxiety, you could try to practice empathy too when your partner is trying to tell you their point of view. When they reassure you and try to show their support, don't dismiss them or their suggestions before thinking about it from an empathetic perspective.

Above all else, when communicating with each other, take the time to remind each other of your love. Use that love as the strength you need to overcome this hurdle. Anxiety can only get the best of your relationship if you allow it to happen. If you happen to be the one playing the supportive role in the relationship for your anxious partner, remind them that you are not going anywhere and if they need someone to talk to, encourage them to trust you enough to open up. This may take some time though and a lot of persuasions, so you are going to need to exercise a fair amount of patience here to help them through the process.

Conclusion

Your relationships are worth fighting for, not just your romantic relationships, but any relationship that matters in your life. A relationship should make you fill happy and fulfilled, and it will, once you have conquered your anxiety for good. Think about what life would be like once anxiety is no longer in the picture. The freedom from always worrying that your partner is going to leave, freedom from thinking that you are not worth loving. Freedom from the sleepless night that have kept you up for so long because your anxious mind won't turn off. Imagine how much better your relationships will be because anxiety is no longer a consistent burden to bear.

Overcoming anxiety is a journey. Like all journeys, it is going to push you to your limits and test you to your breaking point. You're going to cry, be frustrated, feel like giving up at times, but the one thing you can hold on to is that it will get better. Lean on the strength of the relationships you have around you, your family, friends, and especially your partner. Once you overcome anxiety, it is going to be worth all the struggle you had to go through.

You know that you don't want live with anxiety for the rest of your life. You know that you don't want it to affect your relationship any longer, and that is why you chose to make it to the end of this book. You have the tools you need to get started, but if any point you do feel like you need professional help, never be afraid to ask for help. It is okay to admit that you need help sometimes.